C000125687

The most successful housewives are blessed
with an inspired laziness.

Halving the Housework

For those who hate doing it

Copper Beech Publishing

Published in Great Britain by Copper Beech Publishing Ltd
This edition © Copper Beech Publishing Ltd 2012

ISBN 978-1-898617-50-1
A CIP catalogue record for this book is available from
The British Library.

Copper Beech Gift Books
Copper Beech Publishing Ltd
East Grinstead Sussex England

... keep your workspace
clear of clutter

Clear muddle and clutter
What to remove
Making a timetable
How-to-do-it drills
Advice on spring cleaning
What not to iron
Lazy tips

INTRODUCTION TO HOUSEWORK

There may be women who actually like housework. But most – let's be honest – hate housework. It's dull; it's boring. It demands a certain degree of concentration, but not enough to make it a satisfying job of work.

This book is dedicated to anyone who believes that there is no virtue in household drudgery.

Exclusive devotion to the removal of dust can be a vice.

They use their brains as well as their hands – and their hands are fit to be seen when they play hostess. Instead of searching for more work, they contrive ways of making some of the work unnecessary. For the rest, they use modern methods, quite disregarding Aunt Gertrude's dictum that the only way is hands-and-knees-and-plenty-of-elbow-grease. There is no magic wand, no button that can be pressed and hey presto! Everything's perfect.

A cocktail party means extra washing up, and a baby at some period of his life is quite certain to decide to wear his laden dinner-plate, upside down, as a hat.

Chores have to be done. But they don't have to be done the hard way, and they don't need to be added to. Treat the whole dull business on a rational basis, and you can cut down both the time and labour spent on it. If you're coming completely new to the job, then follow this guide as carefully as you'd follow a new recipe; in time you'll cut down both the chores and the hours spent on them by about half.

The first part deals with streamlining. Then, if you go round the home, book in hand, and compare each of the rooms with the recommendations made you'll see exactly which fits your particular kind of home – and how the mass of chores could be reduced.

Make as many of the changes as your conscience and sentiment permit. It may mean being fairly ruthless. Shed a tear, if you like, over the old favourite encumbrances and muddle-makers. But throw them out just the same.

The second part of the guide deals with the new ways of getting through the fewer chores which still remain to be done. You may need the book in front of you when you start, if you haven't tried these ways before. But they'll soon become second nature, done without thinking.

There's one extremely important point to be mentioned. You're starting off on the wrong foot if you try to 'make do' with inadequate equipment, or put off buying what you need in this direction. Make sure you have the proper equipment.

STREAMLINING THE HOME DECKS

You can't work quickly in muddle and clutter. The old saw about 'a place for everything and everything in its place' still goes today, and even more so in a small, modern home. Unfortunately, that's where there often isn't enough space for everything. If you accept this in a spirit of patient resignation, then you'll go on moving things to get at other things, picking them up and putting them down in new places, walking quite unnecessary distances, and doing more dusting than you need.

Stow away

You can, for one thing, stow away. The dusting of a cupboard, plus, say, a thrice-yearly turn-out, takes far fewer hours than daily dusting of the fifty or more objects contained in it.

Stowing away must be treated with circumspection, otherwise it becomes a pernicious habit.

Take a firm line

Only what is really needed should be around in the home, and it is necessary to take a firm line both with yourself and the rest of the family on this point.

Too much stowing of the wrong things brings moths and mice and mess.

Clutter

A home is exactly like a cupboard, once you give way to hoarding. Occasional clutter of someone doing a bit of carpentry, or the necessary mending basket is quite different from when people – quite reasonable people – hoard gift ornaments and early furnishing mistakes and broken-down chairs; they hoard ugly things for sentimental reasons and unnecessary things because they've never thought of getting rid of them, or because 'the place wouldn't look the same without them'.

Hoarding

These people hoard dust-collectors and work-makers and shin-bumpers. This applies more to the ten-year-old home than to the new one that's just beginning. But even starting off you need to be careful. It's only too easy to buy too much at the outset and then to find that some early (and possibly quite expensive) buys weren't needed at all.

This is the very stuff of which hoarding is made. Before you know where you are, the clutter is collecting.

Throwing out ...

The first step – throwing out

So throw out (or stow) anything that isn't really doing a worthwhile job around the house. Your rooms will certainly benefit. One of the biggest differences, once you come to think of it, between the over-full, bulging-walled Victorian home and the clean-lined 'contemporary' kind you admire in the photographs in the 'glossies' is simply the amount to be found in the room.

An objective manner

Look at your possessions dispassionately. After that, go round the place, book in hand, and do some mental arithmetic. The computation is very simple. Just total the number of objects, minus the number of objects unnecessary, unbeautiful, unhygienic, untrustworthy, unserviceable, unwanted. If you find your determination wavering, call in the help of a caustic-minded friend who can be trusted to speak plainly. Above all, look at things in an objective manner, or as objective as possible under the circumstances.

Look at your home as if you were a stranger, seeing your home for the first time.

What to consider in the operation 'Throw Out'
You won't be able, for a number of reasons, to discard everything - sentiment, Aunt Agatha's possible legacy, the landlord's certain disapproval, economic pressure, can all militate against a complete and perfect streamlining.

You can do more than you first suppose, once you really set your mind to the job.

Remove odd bits of furniture
This includes 'extra' chairs standing in hall-ways or just inside doors; 'occasional tables' for the use of which no occasion arises; hall-stands that collect coats in unsightly huddles. (If you want somewhere to stow away coats and umbrellas, put them in a cupboard, which is a much more streamlined piece of furniture. If you haven't a cupboard, buy one second-hand if necessary, or make one.)

These objects, and a number of others, are expendable. So are chairs with stuffing coming out (sometimes put to be 'used up' in the kitchen, though never sat on, just something more to be walked round); and tables with a broken leg, old bedsteads long discarded for sleeping, but taking up room in the loft, boxroom or shed which could be must better employed housing something that really can't be thrown away.

Remove bric-a-brac

You don't need to strip the place. Just take away about three-quarters of the things crowded on shelf and mantel, window-sill and small table, piano and desk and sideboard. Leave a choice few. They'll show up much better by standing singly, as well as causing much less dusting.

Aunt Agatha's china dogs (sentiment or legacy) could go into a trunk until she visits you, and later until such time as the little antique shop decides that they are recherché and will give you a really good price for them.

Leave a choice few pieces

Remove things from walls

This includes small oval, or round mirrors that do nothing but reflect a patch of paper on the opposite wall; pictures that nobody ever thinks of looking at; framed photographs of innumerable relatives and of your wedding day. There's no need to have bare walls. Leave one or two things — like ornaments, a really good picture. What remains will show up all the better for having lots of space around it.

Newspapers

Remove newspaper and magazine collections. Anything over a week old. You won't ever get round to reading them now.

Remove things that 'may come in useful'. They won't, otherwise you would be using them. While they're waiting, they collect moth and dust.

Rugs

Remove bits of rugs lying on top of other carpeting. 'Slip mats' outside doors may have gone out of fashion, but there are still plenty of equivalents – hearth-rugs; bedside rugs (which aren't needed if there's already a carpet); rugs in the hall, where the dog pelts downstairs and slides on. Cover the floors completely from wall to wall and you won't need rugs. Linoleum, needleloom, sisal and 'tufted' carpeting are inexpensive if you can't run to wool carpeting.

If you can't afford any of these, then stain and polish the boards, and lay rugs direct on them. They don't cause as much work as they do when lying on top of carpet.

Look at the following picture.
What would you remove to save cleaning chores?

Remove picture-rails

They make the place look old-fashioned and aren't, or certainly shouldn't be, used for hanging pictures (invisible hooks behind the pictures are much better). And they are unnecessary causes of extra reaching-up dusting.

Remove all brown paint

If you want to be able to skip a day's chores now and then, choose pale colours for woodwork. There's no need to feel limited in your choice – white, off-white, peach, lilac, delicate apple green are all perfectly suitable for inspired laziness.

Remove the empty coal scuttle during the summer
Left in its usual place it simply acts as a second waste-paper basket, collecting cigarette ends and ash and crumpled envelopes, which leaves you with the alternatives of enduring the untidy look or of doing a double emptying job every day.

Frills and flounces

Remove frills, flounces, cummerbunds, all odd bits of curtaining of any kind which do not shake easily free from dust, and are just as easily taken down for dunking. Places you're most likely to find these are: around lampshades; hiding a clutter of raincoats which hang from an overhead shelf; below the draining-board, supposedly hiding the pails (what's the matter with making a hardboard door? – not a difficult thing); as elaborate frills, double-tiered, round beds and cots (look wonderful in shops, but how about getting them off when they look grubby?); beautiful, deep, dust-collecting box-pleats on bottom edges of 'loose covers'.

Window covers are a necessity, as well as being an important part of a room's furnishings, but unless you're very much overlooked by neighbours, there's no particular reason for an extra half-curtaining of net as well. Dressing-table 'petticoats' can get by. But make them in such a way that they can be easily taken off for washing.

Bits and pieces

Remove boxes, oddments, bits and pieces, old letters stuck behind ornaments, things that stand on tables because nobody ever thinks of taking them away, any small vessel that can be filled with left-over pins, lighter flints, snapshots, money, tickets; any larger box containing snippets left over after making curtains, frocks and bedspreads.

If you must keep these left-over bits and pieces, then put them in a cupboard. If you haven't a suitable storage place, then make one.

Remove bulbous pink silk lampshades
They are unbeautiful, unfashionable and nearly always unclean, because, whether or not you dust them, grime just works its way into the fabric, and there's nothing you can do about it.

Gramophone records
Remove gramophone records to a safe and enclosed place, as well as covering up the gramophone whenever it's not in use. Both records and machine are terrible dust-collectors, with any number of small ridges, grooves, lumps and excrescences which demand separate and careful dusting, not to mention covers which are practically unreachable. Further to this point, when you go along to help in the buying of a new radio, refuse firmly to be side-tracked by unimportant matters like VHF and self-determining oscillation, but go all out for the machine with the fewest crenellations and interstices – the one which won't be impossible to dust. Chances are you'll get the best reception this way in any case; makers of good sets are equally interested in good exterior design.

Plants

Remove indoor plants from indoors to outdoors any time there's a warm and gentle shower. This way you'll get them washed without any trouble. Dust doesn't become them; besides which, it clogs the leaf-pores and causes the plant to die off.

Shoes

Remove shoe collections from floors. Buy shoe-racks to keep them tidy and prevent fluff collection.

A cluttered huddle isn't pretty. It's one of the unsuspected reasons why housewives sometimes want to leave home.

PUSHING THINGS AROUND

Once you're rid of the junk, the next step is to examine what's left and see how you can use it to the best effect with the least effort.

Have you ever tried pushing furniture around in a room, changing the positions of the big and important pieces? You'd be surprised at the different look you can give the place – this, as well as the amount of time you can save in keeping it clean and spruce.

Homely, inviting and comfortable

There's another reason for the lay-out of the furniture – to make rooms look easy, inviting and comfortable. You don't have to sacrifice these essential, homely qualities. Streamlining for easy work runs hand in hand with appearance.

A cluttered huddle

A cluttered huddle isn't pretty. It robs a room of any character, because you simply don't notice anything in particular, only a mass of furniture. It's also one of the unsuspected reasons why housewives sometimes want to leave home. But a single chair, islanded on a sea of carpet, shows up as a note on its own, as well as being much easier to get around and dust.

A fireside grouping

This doesn't mean you can't have easy-chairs and sofa comfortably grouped round the fire. In fact, it's probably the best place, not only for warmth, but also for easy working. Fireplace and door are nearly always on different walls. So fireside grouping means you don't have the big furniture getting in the way as you come into the room armed with carpet sweeper or vacuum cleaner (or tea-trolley).

Streamlining

Streamlining doesn't mean putting everything round the walls, leaving the middle of the room bare, either. This wouldn't even save chores, because the wall-pieces would have to be moved for dusting.

Put things where they're needed, but well spaced out – so that you can get round and under and over without having to reach and bend and move every time you want to clean. Look sternly and critically at every bit of your home. Is there a recess completely filled by a chair, close up to a table, flanked on the other side by yet another chair? If so, you're either harbouring dust or doing a lot of unnecessary moving when you clean.

Some of the villains

Have you an 'occasional table' for which the only place is a corner behind a big and heavy settee? And do you dust it every day by kneeling on the settee – or by pushing the settee out?

Are there chairs parked in a smallish hall (making it look smaller still), which are in the way when you walk through, and which bark your shins as you carry large, view-impeding armfuls of clean laundry upstairs after ironing? These are some of the villains of the housework drama, but do something more than curse them.

BEDROOM LAY-OUTS

Try to forget the conventional lay-outs. Beds, traditionally, are set with their heads against a wall, the rest of them sticking out straight and uncomprisingly into the middle of the room.

Put the bed side-on to the wall, and certainly you'll have to pull it out every day for making. But if you give it big, easy-run castors, this 'once-out once-back' push may mean very much less trouble than the amount of extra walking you do circling round the bed every time you go into the room.

the conventional lay-out ...

THE DINING ROOM

Apply the same thoughts to a table in the middle of the dining-room. Colliding and avoiding takes time. A table at one end, or to one side (it doesn't have to stand flush to the wall), can mean getting in and getting out, and cleaning the floor without any extra and unnecessary movements. So just start pushing. Even if you spend a whole morning re-distributing furniture, and don't get any cleaning done at all, you're practically certain to gain in the end.

Making it difficult

Chairs in front of cupboards which are constantly in use; or behind doors constantly opened; a heavy desk planted firmly into a bay window, making it difficult for you to open and shut the windows, or shake the curtains free of dust (the quick and easy way to keep them clean); anything that has to be shifted to get at something else; move these things once and for all into places where they don't make nuisances of themselves; or do away with them altogether.

The furniture-makers can help

If you like entertaining – parties and friends to stay – but haven't the space to make the room for them or move things into, then you'll need to buy or replace with the kind of furniture that's been made for this kind of home.

There are inexpensive and very modern dining-chairs that can be stacked in a tidy, space-saving manner. There are double-decker bunk beds, or beds that fit on top of each other to form one single. There are tables which, when they're not in use, will fold; or flap upwards and disappear into a wall cupboard; or become smaller, obligingly swallowing their middle leaf.

A fitted window seat can hold toys, or big seasonal-use things like extra blankets and the change of window curtains.

THE KITCHEN

And now to the kitchen – room of rooms, the workshop and powerhouse of the home. It's simply no use moving chairs and table around here. If it isn't planned to make work easy, then you're condemned to spend long hours just walking.

What is needed in the kitchen is streamlining of storage and 'working units' to a properly thought-out plan. This costs money, but it's money well spent.

A choice of three layouts

There is a choice of three layouts, one of which is almost bound to suit your particular kitchen. The basic idea of all of them is a chain link which works from the entrance door, where foods come in (refrigerator or meat safe, vegetable rack, dry-goods cupboard); then to the working surfaces, where you prepare the food; and finally, to the sink, in that order.

Here are the three alternative kitchen plans:

1. To put everything along one long wall.

2. The two-wall or corner treatment.

3. The three-wall or sometimes called the 'horseshoe' arrangement.

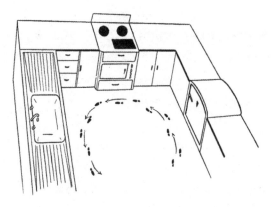

This last is the most practical scheme for the little kitchenette; though it can have its uses, too, in the very large and old-fashioned kitchen. Study your kitchen. It's a good idea to draw out a rough plan of it on paper. Decide which of the three set-ups suits you best.

Backache

Irregular heights and depths not only look untidy but make you bend and straighten each time you move from one to the other, constantly adjusting yourself to different levels – a fine recipe for backache.

Work with the least strain

There's one height, and only one, that is exactly right for you. It will allow you to work with the least strain. Besides this, pieces which don't fit make extra work when you have to get in between them and clean small, awkward places where bits of food have dropped and grease has splashed down from the cooker.

These fitting and matching units can be bought piece by piece. Choose a branded type, and you'll know that later on you can match up with others of exactly the same dimensions.

You can make these units with 'Do-it-Yourself' kits, which cost much less, and need very little skill. They come ready prepared, with all the difficult things like dovetailing and tenon-jointing done for you. There's nothing to do but assemble, sand-down and paint.

A recipe for backache

Scrubbing the walls 1890

Scrubbing is one of the hard chores, which ought by now
to have been completely abolished in
this modern world.

Compare these rooms before and after ...

TOP DRESSING

Once you've got everything in the house properly arranged for quick-get-round working, start looking critically at the surfaces of everything – furniture, furnishings, walls and floors. The Victorians used to say disparagingly that beauty is only skin-deep. Well, the skin or surface of everything in the house makes a big difference to the chores. Some save work, others make it.

You can divide surfaces roughly into two groups:
The kind which will absorb dust, dirt, water and stains, and
the kind that won't.

Surfaces

All through the house the best thing to have as far as you can is the non-absorbent kind of surface. In the kitchen it's an absolute necessity. And yet …

Think for a moment of wood – in its plain, unvarnished, unpainted form, stainable, wettable, dirt-absorbing. You don't find it in this form in the sitting-room and the bedroom. But in the kitchen it's still used for draining-boards. They're constantly being wetted, so they warp and split, leak driplets on the floor, and eventually they become slimy and rot away.

Scrubbing

Wood is there again, far too often, as a kitchen table and a kitchen floor. All this needs scrubbing to keep it clean. Scrubbing isn't good for anything – least of all wood. Gradually the cellulose between the wood grain is dissolved away, leaving a series of ridged grooves, which simply lap up the dirt.

Nor is scrubbing good for you. It's one of the hard chores, which ought by now to have been completely abolished in this modern world. It's not only bad for wood, but also for fabrics and carpets, and it disturbs the surface of paintwork.

The old-fashioned earthenware sink, which you'll still find accompanying the wooden drainer, is a nuisance, too. It chips and crazes and discolours, and has to be constantly attented to with chloride of lime to keep it in any semblance of whiteness.

You can now buy a combined sink-and-drainer, enamelled or plastic. These cost about the same as a radio set.

How to cut out the hard work

The only way to cut out the hard cleaning work in the kitchen is to make sure that all the surfaces are waterproof, stainproof and greaseproof, as heat resistant as possible, and easily wiped clean of anything that's spilt or splashed.

Bright and gay

Kitchens ought to be bright and gay – we spend hours every day in them, and the work is twice as hard when it's done in dreary surroundings. The 'Do-It-Yourself' redecoration takes a certain amount of time and labour. But once you've got easy-clean surfaces, you'll make back that time and labour many times.

WALLS

Easy-clean walls

For the rest of the walls you've a choice of several kinds of coverings, all of which you can wipe down with one of those little foam-sponge mops on a long handle.

If the room's not too steamy, you could have wallpaper with a wipeable surface. They're made in really good designs these days, and are just the thing if you're using part of the kitchen as a dining-room or breakfast corner. A high-gloss wall surface is inclined to encourage condensation if the room is cold. But there are semi-gloss, matt and flat paints, which are much less likely to make the walls 'run'; some emulsion paints (but find out if the makers actually advise their brand for use in the kitchen); and even, for really bad cases, special "anti-condensation" paints.

Finger marks

Matt or flat paints are fine for walls, but they don't make for easy work on door and mantelpieces, places which are constantly being touched.

You can't stop people making finger-marks, but you can make the marks easy to remove. If you don't like the high shine of full gloss or "enamel" paint, the semi-gloss is just as good, and you can get it in the most wonderful colours in the new opalescent and eggshell paints. They all give a "sealed" surface that comes clean as soon as it's in contact with a damp rag.

Kitchen walls aren't the only ones that collect grime. Mostly in other rooms you don't have to bother very much – an occasional brush-down is all that's needed.

Those extra-grubby spots

But there are odd spots on walls that get extra-grubby:
The part round the electric light switch, a jutting corner
that's constantly touched, the wall behind a divan, where
a head touches when you're reading in bed.

Spongeable wallpapers make things easy in places like this.
But if you've got the ordinary kind of wallpaper, paint these
bits with a transparent film which won't alter the look of
the paper at all, but makes it wipeable.

FACTS ABOUT FLOORS

Linoleum fits the bill. Wood doesn't. Thermoplastic tiles are fine – either a professionally laid floor or 'Do-It-Yourself' tiles that you can stick on practically any surface that's already there, even concrete, if there's no rising damp. Felt-based plastic has a moppable surface, and gives a pleasant soft tread underfoot. You can stick or tack it down.

Stop all that nonsense

There's no need to endure the awful chore of dusting concrete flooring. Even if you can't cover it with tiling, there are sealers in plenty, some coloured, which stop all that nonsense, and will last a year or more before having to be renewed.

Care with bright colours

One point about choosing linoleum or plastic, and it goes for halls and passage-ways as well as kitchens. Plain, solid colours look wonderful, especially in the new brilliant hues that are being made nowadays, but every mark shows – splashed liquid or dust from a rubber-soled shoe.

Once-a-day cleaning is enough for any floor – and there are occasions when you want to skip even that. So if you want an all-over colour, go for the type that's 'flashed' or marbled, or 'jaspe' – muted patternings that don't alter the fundamental hue, but which distract the eye so that the odd mark doesn't stand out for notice.

BUYING CURTAINS

It doesn't matter if you're just married or if you've got a ten-year-old home: you're still going to be buying curtains and upholstery fabrics, bed covers and sheets, at some time. So whether it's first-buy or replacement, the same thing goes – buy for easy work as well as good looks.

PVC sheeting is delightful

Cheap and cheerful for kitchen and bathroom curtaining – places which get all steamed up – is PVC plastic sheeting. It's made in quite delightful colours and patterns, and you can wipe off dirt without even taking the curtains down.

Don't be put off by people who tell you that it rots under strong sunlight. So does any curtain fabric. At around two-and-elevenpence a yard you can afford to replace – and who wants curtains to last for ever, anyway?

Towelling

Terry towelling for bathroom curtains is one of the most easily dunked fabrics, and it doesn't need ironing. Nor do the cottons labelled 'no iron'.

One of the things that make for a clean home with the minimum of effort is immediate attention to spills and splashes. Leave them to dry and they become well settled in, and you'll have a hard job removing the stain.

Terylene doesn't rot

Terylene net is another curtaining. On an economy note, it doesn't rot, even in sea air. (Money-saving note: linings help to keep the room warmer on frosty nights, and protect expensive curtaining from the sun-rays; also, they don't show the dirt, so you needn't wash so often.) Don't let curtain washing become a fetish. Leave the things alone until you see they really need it.

SILICONED PLASTICS

If you're prepared to do-it-now whenever there's a spilling catastrophe, then the upholstery for you is the siliconed fabric. Some furniture is already covered this way; or you can buy the fabric by the yard.

An invisible protection

Siliconing doesn't alter the appearance or the softness of a fabric. It simply adds an invisible protective finish, making the cloth resistant to water-based staining – wine and tea spills, coffee and ink. Gives it, in fact, a sealed surface up to a point. It becomes resistant, though not absolutely proofed. But if you blot and mop at once with clean water you wouldn't know that anything had ever happened.

Plastic upholstery materials have a really sealed non-absorbent surface. There's something to be said for their use on dining-chairs, especially when there are jammy fingers about.

WEDDING PRESENTS

You may not be able to acquire everything you need right away — but you can set a goal and keep adding to the equipment bit by bit. Kind friends and family are sophisticatedly realistic nowadays about wedding presents.

Write a list

Some big department stores have a wedding-present book in which you can write your list of requirements, where all and sundry may read, and cross off what they're going to give you. There's no reason why you shouldn't hopefully include the vacuum cleaner and a refrigerator.

Utensils for easy home-cleaning

One of the first rules for easy home-cleaning is that you shouldn't transfer grime from one place to another, by way of the utensils you are using. If you have a fire-grate to brush out every day in the winter, buy a second cheaper brush (fibre would do), and keep it specially for this job. It doesn't matter then if it gets dirty and stays that way.

THE RIGHT WEAPONS FOR THE JOB

A wet cloth won't do everything. You have to deal with surfaces like carpets which, though they're not born dirty, absorb dirt and bits of grit. There are fibres which aren't siliconed, and which acquire grease and grime with open arms; clothing and table and bed-linen, and most curtains; and flat surfaces, like polished floors and linoleum, which, though they may not absorb, can have dust and mud thrust upon them.

*Given the right tools, you can finish the jobs in a very much
shorter working week, and still have a home which
is far cleaner than homes used to be in
the tiresome good old days!*

First needs for a much smaller price

First needs are a long broom, a short-handled brush and a dustpan. If you buy these in plastic – nylon brushes, high impact polystyrene dustbin – you'll be able to wash them without trouble.

You'll want a carpet sweeper – or one of those non-electric suction cleaners, which will do double duty as carpet sweeper and cleaner. They won't do everything an electric vacuum cleaner does, but they do a good job on carpet and lino for a much smaller price.

Cobwebs on the ceiling

A ceiling brush is needed for cobwebs on the ceiling (even in the best of homes!) and for a quick brush-down of walls. Buy the kind with a telescopic handle, and you'll find it easier for carrying round the house. You can also use it in the shortened form as the easiest possible way of dusting skirting boards and the tops of doors.

A feather mop is important.

Use a feather mop when you don't want to take everything off the dressing-table; for the tops of books in a bookcase, and for all of the places where dust shows. Always use it for delicate lampshades. Dust lifted with a feathery flick won't hurt them. Do the job with a cloth, and you simply rub the dust in.

Books are dreadful fluff collectors, and a source of shame when a guest takes a volume out for reference.

Polished floors

You should have a polisher if you have polished floors. It doesn't have to be electric. There are other types that do an efficient job, such as the one with a long handle and lambswool on its end. You fix a bonnet over the pad when you're applying the polish, then you take it off and use the wool for buffing. Any of these save backache and split nylons – and besides, you don't have to wear your oldest skirt and apologise if somebody comes to the door.

Kitchen floors

A sponge mop on a long handle. These are all designed to save you from having to squeeze with bare hands. Some bend in half lengthways, some across their width.

You need this for damp-mopping of the kitchen and, sometimes, for lino, polished surrounds and tiles, to clean up splashes or muddy footmarks. They all do a wonderful job, saving any amount of bending, and they can be seized and used for spills even when you're in the middle of cooking.

Vacuum cleaner

You'll have to have a vacuum cleaner sooner or later. Other things which get into carpets are tiny specks of grit, some almost too small to be seen by the human eye, but not too small to damage the carpet. You can't stop these things coming in on people's shoes. But you can suck them out of the pile of the carpet, before they cause threadbare patches by biting the threads every time anybody walks on them.

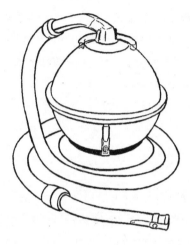

A vacuum cleaner has attachments which get into places you simply can't reach properly with any other weapons.

It's not an extravagance

It's time a refrigerator became an accepted piece of equipment in every home, as necessary as the cooker. It's not an extravagance. It's the proper, hygienic way of keeping food. It also cuts down the number of shopping days, because you can buy and store with certainty. Even the coldest of larders isn't a substitute.

Rub-a-dub-dub, two hands in a tub eventually means backache, when you come to the chore of a family wash. Some washing machines heat their own water; most are filled and emptied 'mechanically' without having to use pails.

Wash when it suits you

A spin-dryer means you're not tied to a fine day (and who wants to start laundry operations on a fine day, anyway?) but can wash just when it suits you.

The spinner is used to extract the suds immediately after the wash, with no need for wringing; and then for both rinsings as well. Fine light materials, like nylon, come out almost dry; heavier fabrics at exactly ironing-damp. It even brings a blanket to the airing stage in about four minutes. Spin-drying doesn't harm buttons and buckles; it can't split rayon threads or make a zipper cut into a dress.

Hot water

You simply must have hot water in abundance for all household chores: washing clothes; washing up; wet-mopping floors; washing of all kinds. Without it, you're always working at a disadvantage. If you haven't a good supply on tap at the sink, then have one put in — sink heater, multi-point, gas or electric storage heater.

Don't ever think you can run the home efficiently armed
with only a kettle and a boiler fire that's put on
just for baths.

Won't chip the best china
Pedal bin, wash-up bowl, pail. Insist that they shall be made of polythene, which is easy to clean, light to carry, doesn't clank noisily and won't chip the best china.

Kitchen gadgetry. If there's something which does the job for you better or more easily, more quickly than you're doing it now, then buy it. But be quite certain:

a)   that you definitely need it and will use it, and
b)   that it hasn't got a mass of difficult bits to clean, parts you can't get at unless you dig with a skewer.

Slick kitchen utensils can save hours in a week
Jugs, handles, spouts and lips can all make extra work if they're not properly designed to avoid it; so can unnecessary ornament and ridging, and narrow necks that defy entry with the wash-up mop.

You can buy kitchen scissors with certainty that they will be used and useful. Give them two hooks if you hang them on the wall, or use their own tin case; hanging open from a single hook, the blades could be dangerous.

THE LIFE OF THE COOKER

A word about the cooker. If it's new and efficient, so much the better. If not, then it needs to be replaced. The life of a cooker should be ten to twelve years. They'll last much longer, but you're not getting the best from them.

Separate electric equipment

There's a good case to be made for separate pieces of electric equipment, like mixer and frying-pan, toaster, kettle and coffee percolator – if you have the need for them. If not, don't buy them. Just buy what you're going to use.

Keep the kitchen streamlined. Try to avoid things with bumps, lumps and horrid little grime-collecting crevices.

When buying a cooker, watch these points

Has it enough burners or hot-plates for present and likely future needs?

Is the "floor" of the hot cupboard (the part between oven top and hob) recessed enough to hold spillings without emptying them straight on to the floor?

Are the grill pan and grid easy to clean?

Is the oven easy to get into (or has it removable sides) so that you can clean it quickly?

Is the oven big enough to be economical – can you pack in a roast, a pie and one or two other dishes for later?

Has the oven enough supports for you to change the shelves to all positions you're likely to need?

Would it be worth your while having automatic oven control, which presents you with a meal cooked and ready to eat, even if you've been out all day?

This does not complete the list of tools for the job. Pressure cookers cut down cooking time enormously, and save fuel, too.

WHAT TO CLEAN WITH

The way to buy cleaning materials is the exact opposite of the way you choose gadgets. Try out anything in the way of cleaners and polishes as it comes on the market. The chances are somebody has found a new and easier way to doing something, and you'll benefit.

Cleaning materials don't cost a great deal; they're a regular weekly buy, so you can afford to gamble.

An unobtrusive corner

If you can't smother doubts about what a new cleaner will do to your home, then reassure yourself by testing it out first on things which don't matter – on the underside of hems, the unobtrusive corner of a carpet or the wall of the box-room. Something or somewhere which would be of no consequence even it it were harmed.

Inspired laziness means using brains to save muscle-fatigue.
It isn't very tiring to read a few words on
the side of a container.

Neighbours with wonderful ideas

Don't listen to that neighbour, who usually has a quivering feather in her hat, and who always has a wonderful idea of using boot-polish for floors, metal-polish for wooden furniture and nail varnish for everything except her nails.

Make your own decision

Shop with an alert eye and open, receptive mind; you'll find nearly everything already prepared for the different needs in a home. Often there is more than one for each purpose. So try them all out in turn, and stick to the one you like best.

Don't go only by initial cost or the size of packet or bottle. You can often get good stuff wrapped up in cheap little parcels. You can also find things which cost more than others, but which save chores by doing a better and more long-lasting job.

SYNTHETIC DETERGENTS

Synthetic cleaners are in both liquid and powder form, for all kinds of washing jobs. They're produced for the weekly wash, and most, contain fluorescence, which is acted upon by the ultra-violet rays in ordinary daylight and makes things look whiter. They're not really any cleaner. The 'extra whiteness' disappears in the yellow beam of an ordinary electric bulb, because this kind of light doesn't contain ultra-violet rays.

Where synthetics do score especially is in hard-water districts. It's virtually impossible to produce 'soap scum' with them, so the clothes and dishes are cleaner.

Silicone polishes and creams

These are made for wood floors and wood furniture as well as for car bodies. As soon as you've spread out a thin film of wax or cream, the silicones start working to the top. Then they form themselves into a hard, dirt-resistant and shiny surface – all with hardly any need for rubbing and buffing.

Needs no polishing

Floor sealers are transparent liquids which are painted on the floor – wood, lino, concrete, thermoplastic tile – and which form a hard surface *which doesn't have to be polished at all.* A damp mop does all that's needed, and the shine persists.

Some sealers last about six weeks, some up to a year or more. One that isn't transparent is a sealing paint especially evolved for concrete. Choice of colours is limited and rather unsubtle, but it does solve the really hard-work problem of a dusty concrete floor. This paint lasts, even under hard treading, for a couple of years.

Metal polishers

Both for brass and silver there are the old tried-and-trusted polishes and there are newer work-savers; for a brass letter box, apply a lacquer after polishing to protect from tarnishing. Another new lacquer is applied to the warming pan and candle sticks; you need only a rub-up with a duster now and then.

If you suspect woodworm in furniture you can polish it with
a silicone cream which is also insecticidal.

Do the job at leisure

Latest oven-cleaner is put on cold. It comes in an aerosol, and a two-second 'burst' with your finger on the button covers the brown burnt-on grease with foam – leave it ten minutes and wipe the oven clean. Means you can do the job at leisure instead of trying to rush it in while you're dishing-up the joint.

Glass cleaners

There are some people who argue that "You can't beat cold water and a chamois leather". But there are now liquids in bottles which you rub on, leave to dry, rub off.

Pictures should never be cleaned with water. Moisture seeps in behind the glass and spoils the mount. Use methylated spirit if you like: it evaporates too quickly to do damage.

Wash-up aids

Wash up with synthetic detergents, either liquid or powder, and you won't have any trouble with grease smears. Measure powder with a teaspoon, not a cup – you know how the packetful suddenly tips in and fills the kitchen with foam.

Scourers

Abrasives, either in powder form in a canister or paste from a tin. These are needed for obstinate marks, usually grease, which can't be moved simply with a damp cloth, and for the soap-line round the bath in hard-water districts.

Do at least a part every day if you can. Or, if you're keeping on your job outside the home and can't manage more, then get down to the whole thing once a week.

ROUTINE IN SWING TIME

If you want a clean and tidy home, and you want it the easy way, then you've got to get rhythm. Dash around the place in a haphazard fashion, without any plan of campaign, and you have to stop and think between chores. This takes time. And if you haven't a clear idea of just what you mean to do that morning you're very likely to leave out something important. Later on you have to catch up by doing it in a rush. Which at once brings in a sense of strain. That's not the way to inspired laziness!

You need a timetable

No need to write down every chore in the house and then try to work through the whole lot every day. That's a sure road to alarm and despondency.

Keep it in your head. And if you're a novice at the job start off in a very small way, including nothing but the most urgent priorities.

you've got to get rhythm ...

The 'musts'

Every day you'll have to make beds, produce meals and wash them up. These are musts. So is a bit of washing – either overnight dunking of nylon smalls and drip-drys or, if you prefer, a weekly launder-and-iron. And to this add a bit of floor cleaning (a carpet sweeper and mop will do for the first week or so) and some dusting. Town houses get much dirtier than country ones.

Running like clock-work

When you get the first part of your programme running like clock-work, and you've cut down the time you take, you can begin adding in some of the other chores in strict order of priority. You may not have noticed it, but by now dust is beginning to collect on above-eye-level places, like the tops of cupboards and wardrobes, and doors and window-frames, and behind and underneath things that can't be moved often.

No need to panic

There's no need to panic over this. You'll never be able to

clean them all every day, nor even every week. All they need is periodic attention, so that everything in the house is dusted, or washed, or polished, or swept at some time.

Regular 'turn-outs'

If you do one room every week, and take a little trouble over it, it'll stay clean for quite a while. Bedroom one week, sitting-room next, kitchen the third and so on. Just work them in an orderly fashion, and they'll slip into place without trouble.

Now take a long breath and look round for the other chores in your home. The regular turn-outs help a lot, even if each room is done only once in four, five or six weeks, but –

There are some things that can't be left waiting so long. You need to clean the oven after a roast, take a damp cloth to fingermarks on the paint and do some extra polishing – furniture, windows, mirrors, floors and, perhaps, ornamental brasses and silver, and a doorstep. Work them all in, using your head and the newest and most helpful accessories and cleaners.

Running smoothly

If you're coming new to all this it'll probably take you about six months to establish your routine and get it running smoothly.

Routines can get interrupted

Housework, no matter how perfect your routine, gets interrupted – by emergencies, major or minor. Spills and splashes must be attended to at once, even if you don't get the windows cleaned that morning.

If the boss is coming to dinner (well, anyway, someone you want to impress) you'll need the time you meant to spend turning out, for shopping and cooking, instead.

The extraordinary plumbing of English homes can lead to water getting in the wrong places at any time of the year.

There isn't any sense in dusting the piano every day if you discover that it doesn't tell tales when you miss a day.

Here are a few important things to remember:

1. It takes no longer to remove the dust of two or three days than that of just one. Grime left to accumulate for a whole year in an out-of-the-way place may mean hard scrubbing.

2. Homes are less important than people. A rigid timetable puts the emphasis the wrong way round.

Don't be chained to chores when there's the combination of husband and holiday or family and fine day as a possible alternative. Enjoy their company on a scratch picnic. They'll enjoy yours if you give them the chance.

3. Monday is a bad day for washing. Slack up on the ordinary housework over the week-end. Laundering takes time, even though it isn't the hard work it once was. So spruce house on Monday, wash on Tuesday and take up the chores again on Wednesday.

4. Saturday is a bad day for shopping. Too many people choose it, which means waiting around and wasting time. Buy that refrigerator and do week-end shopping on Friday. Afternoon is usually better than morning.

5. Don't be hidebound about a Sunday mid-day roast — what's the matter with a cold meal which doesn't involve so much preparation and washing-up, and leaves you the afternoon free to spend in the garden? You can have a roast any night of the week with much less trouble.

6. Be firm about spring cleaning. DON'T DO IT! And don't be apologetic about it either. Now-and-then attention to everything throughout the year keeps the home much cleaner than any seasonal onslaught involving unnecessary hard work, inconvenience and discomfort.

A chubby baby means a skeleton housework routine.
Don't worry about this. Remember that tarnished silver can
be restored to brilliance after months of neglect.
A missed play-hour is lost for ever.

HOW-TO-DO-IT DRILLS
TURNING OUT A ROOM

You will take an entire morning if you go at this haphazardly, a lot of time wasted by unnecessary trailing about, and you'll probably end up feeling tired and depressed. What you want after all that work is a glow of triumph, a satisfaction in a room that looks shining and cared-for; and the pleasant knowledge that it'll go on looking that way for quite a while, without a lot of extra attention.

Logical

Work through in a logical order, and the job shouldn't take more than an hour and a half, if the room is a small one, and you've adopted the streamlining method.

A quick mop-and-dust

Get the beds made, the washing-up out of the way, and do a quick mop-and-dust of the other rooms first, so that you needn't keep worrying about the rest of the house looking untidy. Rub barrier cream into your hands, and start in.

Wasted time and energy

Collect everything you're going to need. Extra walks to and from the cupboard where you keep brooms and brushes, and to the kitchen for damp cloths and polishes, take up time and use energy to no good purpose.

Equipment you'll need:

The vacuum cleaner, plus the attachments for cleaning pelmet tops, upholstered chairs, and corners

Polish and polisher for surrounds

Feather mop

Ceiling brush

Steps, or step-stool, if there's any high-up paint work or tops of high cupboards to explore

Warm water in a bowl and a clean rag

Glass cleaner and rag

Clean duster and polish for furniture

Once you have got to hand everything you can possibly want shut the door and begin.

Disturb all the dust you can

Use the ceiling brush to explore dark corners where there may be cobwebs; for the tops of door - and window-frames, and the top of the door itself. Go on to brush down the walls (vertical surfaces do collect dust) and run all round the picture rail, if you have one. Shake the curtains well. Flick the lamp shades with the feather mop; do the picture frames with this, too. As you come to each one lift a little away from the wall (no need to take them down), and flick both the picture back and the wall. Cobwebs collect here, also.

Solid-topped pelmets and the tops of cupboards need the dusting nozzle on the vacuum cleaner extension. Use this for bookshelves as well. Take out the books: vacuum them and the empty shelves, and put the books back right away. Stroke down the curtains with the vacuum's upholstery nozzle.

The rest of the dust

You will have got the worst of the loose dust in the vacuum bag, but there'll be some floating about still. Let it settle while you remove small ornaments from shelves and window sills. Dust the ornaments with the duster, or, if they need it, wipe them with a damp cloth (you've got the water there ready). Then put them somewhere safe – in the middle of the dining table, or on the bed, or a settee, so that you've got a clean sweep of the places where they were standing. Dust or wipe the shelves and dust all the rest of the furniture.

Vacuum-clean the carpet, turning back the edges, if it isn't tacked down. These edges, and the part under a bed, where blanket-fluff collects, are an open invitation to moths. Vacuum-clean the top of the skirting board, and the upholstery, getting right down into the sides of easy-chairs.

Wipe paint-work, tiles, window-sills, doors and window-frames, light bulbs, anything that's wipeable – using the damp rag, constantly wrung out in warm water. You'll probably need the steps at this stage.

Polish

Put polish on the surrounds. Let is stay there while you polish the furniture (including the shelves if necessary).

Then come back to the surround and buff. Ten minutes' 'sinking in' for floor polish makes the job easier and more efficient.

Clean the windows and picture glass. Put the ornaments back. You're through!

Time yourself on an uninterrupted run

After doing each room two or three times, you should find that you get through more quickly. You'll also find whether you're including some jobs more frequently than necessary. If windows are cleaned all over the house on a regular two- or three-week basis, you might be able to leave these. But don't forget the picture glass when you're turning out.

On the other hand, if you have ornamental metal – things like warming pans and brasses – it may be easier to do them during the turn-out instead of each week.

High-up paint-work may not get dirty quickly in your district. You could perhaps get by with the ceiling brush for two turn-outs out of every three, keeping the damp cloth just for finger-marks on the door.

If you're pressed for time and can't manage the whole job in one go, concentrate on the less obvious places – corners, both floor and ceiling; above eye-levels; interior of bookshelves. Other things are bound to get some attention in the daily dust-and-mopping.

When you're buying anything – new furniture, curtains, upholstery or polishes – concentrate on easy-clean surfaces. The less receptive they are to grime, the less time they'll take in turning out and in the daily routines.

A word about spring cleaning – DON'T DO IT!

BED-MAKING

Airing

An unstripped mattress is unhygienic and unhealthy. Everything that comes in close contact with our bodies needs thorough airing – shoes, clothes and beds.

Strip the bed as soon as you're out of it. Leave it while you get up and dress and eat breakfast. This gives it time to 'breathe' before you make it.

Plumping pillows

The job takes just under five minutes – including plumpng the pillows, folding nightdress or pyjamas, and final smoothing. If that's better than your record, try and see if you can cut down the time you take.

It should take five minutes to make a bed.

Chilly nights

If your blankets aren't quite wide enough, and let draughts in from the sides on chilly nights, put the first one on the right way. Put the second on the wrong way, with the length across the bed, so that you get a really big tuck-in on each side.

Turning the mattress

Spring mattresses need occasional turnings. Turn from side-to-side alternately with top-to-bottom, to keep the wear even. Get help with this if you can, for it is very important not to bend springs.

Nylon sheets

These are usually 'tailored' to fit the corners of a mattress. Work this fitting-on into the bed-making routine without taking extra time.

These sheets can be washed at home, 'spin dried' and go back on the bed the same day.

HERE IS THE DRILL FOR BED-MAKING

Fling

Take the bedclothes off in order, one piece at a time, and fling them over a chair. They're then all ready, still in the right order, to go back again.

Flap

Have the chair near the foot of the bed, but with space, so that you can pass between it and the bed. Sheets and blankets are longer than they are broad, even in the double size. Work from the foot of the bed; you will have much better control as you lift and flap it on to the bed.

Flatten

Pick the under-blanket off the chair. Take one bound end (across the width) in both hands; stand at the foot of the bed, and flat the blanket upwards. It'll lie smoothly at the foot, but there may be puckers at the head, so you'll have to go up and flatten them.

Seize

As you come back, seize the under-sheet and do the same thing. If you tuck in the under-sheet separately from the top things you won't have it coming out when you open the bed at night.

Plump

Pick up the pillows as you pass the chair, 'plump' them up and throw them to the head of the bed.

Tuck

Flap the top sheet from the foot. After a few tries, you'll get it to lie reasonably flat. Tuck in at the foot, flap on the blankets in the same way.

Pull

Place the pillows in position; pull out any puckers in sheet and blankets; fold the sheet over neatly, and tuck all down the side. Do the same thing up the other side and you're ready to put on eiderdown and coverlet.

If you take off the coverlet carefully every night, folding it down and hanging it over the chair, it can go back the same way without trouble. You'll find it doesn't get unduly grubby, and that it stays spruce for a longer time between washings and pressings.

WASHING

"…. *Washes like a rag*", they tell you cheerfully when you're buying a new cotton dress. But there's more to washing than just dunking clothes in hot lather. Suppose you can wash it easily: has it got to be ironed afterwards? And, does it look like a rag unless you starch and damp down?

In the shop

Start your wash-day in the shop where you're buying clothes, and you'll cut out a lot of work and wasted time. Synthetic materials are washed easily enough and you can buy 'resin finished' cottons and linens which are not only crease-resistant in actual wear, but which need the minimum of ironing. Wool is usually all the better for not being ironed.

Swing tickets

Look especially for tabs, labels and swing tickets on ready-made clothing, giving details about the kind of material, and the way it should be cleaned, or washed and ironed. Don't throw a swing ticket of this kind. Keep it by you and refer to it. It wasn't put there for fun. It was intended to help you. Just write a word or two on the ticket to identify the garment – like 'pink sleeveless', or 'white with blue spots', and hang the tickets on a peg in the wardrobe.

Fast colour

One more word about buying: go always for things that are guaranteed 'fast colour'. If a colour isn't 'fast', then it's 'fugitive', and this means that you get a whole set of complications which add to the time you take in the process of washing, drying and ironing. Any material with a fugitive colour has to be washed all by itself, or you'll stain the other things in the washing machine or the bowl.

Nightly dunkings

In most homes washing goes on most of the week, with small nightly dunkings (usually in the bathroom) of nylons, socks, stockings and underwear. This must happen even if you send all the 'big things,' like sheets, shirts and towels, to the laundry.

If you do most things at home with a big wash-day, it's still a good idea to have little washes as well.

Big weekly and little nightly

The wash should be done in two parts: 'big weekly' (which can cover anything); and 'little nightly'. It makes things easier, and the 'big weekly' is less of a chore when it's not cluttered with a lot of small, quite easily washed underclothing and stockings.

Soaking

You can save trouble (as well as getting your linen cleaner with less soap) if you soak really soiled whites in water overnight. The water must be cold, not hot.

You're then using, although you may not know it, a chemical process called "pedesis", which, put simply, just means that the water percolates gently between fabric and the grime-globules, and pushes the dirt off.

Hot water doesn't do it. It may, in some cases, 'set' stains and marks, making them more difficult, or even impossible, to remove.

Now for the wash

Divide it up while the washing machine is filling or heating. (If you have the kind of machine which has to be filled from a pail, you can cut down the lifting of water by using a hose. Buy a yard or so from the chain store, fit a nozzle and lead in straight from the tap. Or for four-and-eleven you can buy a hose with a "universal" nozzle attached, one that fits on any size of tap.)

The order of washing

There's no reason, with an ordinary and moderate-sized wash, why you shouldn't use the same water all the way through, as long as you're careful about the order of washing. With big things, like blankets, you'll need to change the water, but they're better done on a day when you feel particularly energetic, and all by themselves.

First things to go into the absolutely clean water are table napkins and tea-towels. Keep things which are to do with food, or are touched with the mouth, together, and give them this first, clean washing.

They go into the spin dryer, and then to the first rinsing water while the next batch is put into the machine.

Next can be cotton underwear or sheets. Put the cleanest things in first, the more dirty afterwards.

Two rinsings are enough if you use the spin dryer three times for each batch: to extract the suds (the first, clean suds can go back into the machine, to save water and washing powder), and then after each rinse. To save hot water, you can use the almost clear water from a second rinse to do the first rinsing of the next batch.

Woollen socks

If you want to do woollen socks or school knickers in the machine these will obviously have to go in after the whites have been finished, and when the water's getting cooler.

Hanging up

Hanging up is more important than most people think. You'll never get a tablecloth absolutely squared-up however much you iron, if you don't straighten it out in the wet state. On the other hand, intelligent hanging can actually cut down, or even cut out, some of the ironing.

Nylon underwear

This can be washed just as easily, and should be washed just as often. Leave grime to collect on the back hem of a slip, and it will be almost impossible to remove. If the hem has got thoroughly grimed, and you've got a greyish tinge all over, keep on soaking the slip in successive clean lathers, rinsing and putting it in again. The job can be done, but it's a nuisance and a time-waster. Nightly dunking is much easier.

Socks

One way of cutting down washing chores is to present your menfolk with socks they can wash themselves.

Drip-dries

Drip-dries are the answer to a housewife's prayer. But don't expect miracles. Wash carefully, and hang them dripping wet from a plastic hanger.

Permanent-pleat skirts should be washed by hand, keeping them as straight as possible, not creasing and crumpling the pleat.

Sometimes you have to scrub ...

IRONING

'If a job's worth doing, it's worth doing well.'

However, the most efficient way is usually the quickest and easiest, and has the most lasting results.

There are things that don't need to be done at all. There is no need to iron tea-towels; this is nonsense. Tea-towels are in constant use, and need frequent washing – a couple ought to go into soak at the end of every day, if they're to be kept hygienic. Their span of looking nice is, therefore, confined to the time they spend in the drawer, where nobody sees them.

The same thing applies to towels. 'Just a rough run-over to smooth them.' Why? They go straight into the linen cupboard, and you don't see them until it's their turn to be used. And once you've dried yourself on them, nobody can tell whether or not those ends were pressed.

Do not be bullied, either by other people's disapproval or by your own conscience, into ironing anything just for the sake of saying it's been ironed.

It is possible nowadays to lop entire hours from the time which used to be spent at the ironing board.

NEVER IRON THE FOLLOWING
Towels of all kinds except 'guest towels'
Tea-towels
Terry-towelling curtains
Net curtains
'Folkweave' or any other thick, rough-textured curtains
Nylon underwear (men's and women's)
Socks, stockings and gloves
Wool jumpers, sweaters, cardigans
'Drip-dry' shirts for men, made of synthetics
Any clothing definitely labelled 'No iron'
Men's drip-dry pyjamas

The new semi-stiff men's collar which comes up creaseless and crisp with no starch and no ironing. Plastics, whether rainwear or tablecloths, must not be ironed, or you'll destroy them. Just sponge and wipe.

GOOD IDEAS

Net curtaining

Hang it up at the window still damp, thread a rod through the bottom hem to weight it down and stretch it evenly.

An easier way with sheets

Sheets are big and cumbrous. If washed at home, shake and fold them, while they're still damp. Keep edges level, fold compactly and lay the sheet on the ironing-board; cover with the ironing felt and do the rest of your ironing on top. This way the sheet is ironed without you having to iron it! If you feel extra fussy you can iron direct on the bit along the top hem, but it isn't really necessary.

An easier way with handkerchiefs

Put them through the mangle. As you take them out, flap them into squares, and lay them smoothly on top of each other. Unroll on the board, still in the pile, and iron the top one, using a hot iron to make sure you get the fabric dry. The first two, will take the normal time of ironing, the rest will need no more than ironing into folds.

Ties of the washable kind

You're likely to end in bad trouble with linings and bias cutting if you use ordinary laundering methods on them. Ties shouldn't have a sharp creased edge; they ought to be rounded and springy. Do not iron. Buy a tie form consisting of two long triangles, push these into the tie, moisten them with an old nailbrush (use lather if the tie is dirty as well as creased and rinse off with clear water after, leaving the tie damp). No ironing. Result – a tie in perfect shape.

This ironing advice is simply meant to suggest how you apply streamlined methods to this one-time long and wearisome chore.

Wardrobes

Clothing hanging in wardrobes gets crumpled if too many things are squashed in together. Then you've got to do extra ironing.

Turn light-coloured frocks inside-out before you hang them to prevent them from getting grubby, especially if they're jostling up against a winter coat. If they do collect grubbiness, it willl be on the inside and will not show. This is not a counsel of perfection, simply an expedient where time and space are limited.

Same thing goes for light-coloured jumpers and sweaters. Store them in drawers, in the polythene bags in which you bought them, and they'll stay clean until you want to wear them.

Pressing suits (men's or women's) is a good thing if you want to keep them looking smart. But do not overdo it. Comes a time when the fabric has taken in just about all the atmospheric soot it can manage. If you've left it that long, then you'll be forcing the grime right into the fabric. Regular trips to the cleaners are what these things need.

LAZY 'TIPS'

Buy ready-crushed cooking salt, not blocks. It costs a penny or so more, but saves you having to crush – and sweep up the kitchen floor afterwards.

Make it easy for yourself to lift a cake out of a cake-box where it's been stored, by using the box upside down.

Wear a plastic pinafore, too, or you may have to do a 'spotting' job on your best bib and tucker just before the guests arrive.

If you're stuck with an old black firegrate or boiler that you can't replace with something newer, there are heatproof paints which are better than the constant chore of black leading.

LAZY 'TIPS'

When you're frying chips you can cut down the chance of being hit in the eye with spitting fat, by dropping in a pinch of flour first; for some reason it seems to calm the exuberance.

Deal with the difficulty of not being able to put a good, deep bowl under the mincer mouth by not having a bowl or dish at all – but a polythene bag instead.

LAZY 'TIPS'

Pedal bins and dustbins. Keep them dry. Dampness makes them unpleasant to have around, as well as rotting them. If you drain the sink-strainer well, and then empty it into a newspaper, you'll keep your bins longer. Use one of the disinfectant powders in the dustbin, too, to keep flies away. When you're replacing the pedal bin, have a look at the plastic kind which is so easy to wash out.

EQUIPMENT FOR WASHING UP

A polythene bowl (it can't damage anything that might be banged against the side);
A wash-up liquid, or some washing powder;
A foam mop;
Really hot water on tap;
Really clean towels;
And for aluminium saucepans, steel wool of a fine grade (00, if possible).

Given these, you can get through the wash-up with the minimum of effort and the maximum of shine and cleanliness. This shine is important. It isn't difficult to see if china and pans are clean – if they're not, they look smeary. Smears mean that grease still lingers, and lingering grease collects germs, which lead to illness. If that happens, any time you have saved by a 'quick rinse' under the tap is lost a hundred times over.

FLOORS AND FLOOR COVERINGS

If everybody, guests included, took off their shoes before they came into the house we wouldn't need to trouble very much about floors, excepting to mop up an occasional spill. But things being as they are, dirt – grime and actual grit – is being brought into the place all the time.

Accept the dirt

Floors, therefore, unless you stand sentinel at both back and front doors, armed with a dustpan and mop, are always going to be slightly dirty. Accept this fact with calm cynicism, and you can do things which will prevent the grubbiness from making itself obtrusive.

You've usually got two kinds of surfaces to deal with: carpets, which are rough, and surrounds, which are smooth. "Surrounds" includes everywhere that isn't covered by a carpet – a parquet floor sprinkled with rugs; a room covered with felt-based plastic; polished wood round the edge of a carpet square; linoleum, and even quarry tiles and concrete.

These jobs, or their equivalent, are around in everybody's home. You must make up your own "timetable" – it's up to you to do your own streamlining to fit your own home.

Do not shut your eyes to all the things that you can buy, and the short cuts in routine, that make chores less of a bind. So that you'll never need to remember the sad little requiem:

Twinkle twinkle little chair,
How I wish that you were there,
I polished you so hard each day
That now I've rubbed you right away …

Keep your workspace clear of clutter ...

Halving the Housework was first published as part of a book called 'Halving Your Housework' in 1958 by Mills & Boon. Every effort has been made to trace ownership of the content and if any omission has occurred it is inadvertent and it should be brought to the attention of the publisher.

RECIPES OF VARIOUS KINDS
A 'distressed look' book full of recipes collected by a housekeeper over 100 years ago. Learn how to create a dinner party for ten, bake the household bread, cure its ills and discover money saving hints.

TEA; AN EVERYDAY INDULGENCE
Tea time treats, trivia and tastings.
'There is nothing better than an all-white cloth, embroidered or trimmed with lace.'

HOW TO ENTERTAIN YOUR GUESTS
The very best parlour games.
In 1911, one woman collected these indoor games which you can now enjoy today with your guests.

PARTY BOOK
Many of the ideas here for entertaining and party giving are from days gone by, and will inspire the host and hostess today.

THE LADY'S BOOK OF MANNERS
Instructions showing how to be a perfect lady.
How to talk correctly, common errors corrected, polite
conversation, love, courtship and marriage.

THINGS A GENTLEMAN NEEDS TO KNOW
Over a century of advice for men has been collected here
for your instruction and amusement.

ETIQUETTE FOR GENTLEMEN
THE ETIQUETTE OF MOTORING
ETIQUETTE FOR THE TRAVELLER
DON'TS FOR GARDENERS
RECIPES FOR ROSES
ENGLISH LAVENDER

For your free catalogue containing
these and other titles write to:
Copper Beech Publishing
PO Box 159 East Grinstead Sussex RH19 4FS UK
www.copperbeechpublishing.co.uk

Copper Beech Gift Books
are designed and printed
in Great Britain.